GUIDELINES ON SUBJECT ACCESS TO INDIVIDUAL WORKS OF FICTION, DRAMA, ETC.

Final report of the subcommittee on Subject Acess to
Individual works of Fiction, Drama, Etc., presented June 1989
to the RTSD Subject Analysis Committee

Subcommittee on Subject Acess to Individual Works of Fiction, Drama, etc.
Subject Analysis Committee
Cataloging and Classification Section
Resources and Technical Services Division
American Library Association
Chicago and London
1990

Barbra Berman
Bob Ihrig
Pat Luthin
Martha Yee
Liz Bishoff, Chair

The paper used in this publication meets the minimum requirements of American National Standard for Information Sciences – Permanence of Paper for Printed Library Materials, ANSI Z39. 48-1984
Text designed by Barbara McCarty
Composed in Times Roman and Franklin Gothic on a Linotronic, L300 by Coventry Creative Graphics, Inc.
Printed on 50# Cougar, a pH-neutral stock, bound in 10pt. Carolina Coated Cover, by M&D Printing.

ISBN: 0-8389-3386-6

Printed in the United States of America

94 93 92 91 5 4 3 2 1

CONTENTS

Introduction 1

I.   Form/genre access 4

II.   Character access 28

III.   Setting access 32

IV.   Topical access 33

Appendix   Bibliography of reference sources for fictitious
                character and place names 34

Introduction

The following guidelines, prepared and endorsed by the American Library Association's Subject Analysis Committee, constitute a recommendation for national standard practice in the provision of subject access to individual works of fiction, drama, poetry, humor, and folklore in all formats. At the time of publication, these guidelines differ in some respects from Library of Congress practice. The Committee is concurrently recommending these guidelines to the Library of Congress. For improved national access to fiction, we urge the guidelines acceptance by other libraries, even if the Library of Congress is not able to adopt them. They provide an opportunity for libraries that are committed to better subject access to fiction for their users, and that are willing to undertake the extra file maintenance this entails, to provide this access in a standard way, and, thus, to share the cataloging effort among themselves. We have tried to indicate in these guidelines when actual headings recommended here do not appear in *Library of Congress Subject Headings (LCSH)*. If you assign a subject heading that is not in *LCSH*, you should put it in a 690 field in the MARC format. If you assign a genre or form heading from these *Guidelines* that is not in *LCSH,* you should put it in a 655 field, second indicator 7, with the appropriate subfield ≠2 code that identifies this list as the source. (At the time of publication, LC has not yet assigned a code for this list, but when established, it will be published in the list of such codes that is part of the *MARC Format for Bibliographic Data* issued by the Cataloging Distribution Service at the Library of Congress.)

The guidelines are intended to apply only to *individual* works of fiction, drama, poetry, humor, and folklore. For collections by one or several authors, or for literary criticism, consult the Library of Congress subject manual.[1]

---

1 Library of Congress, Subject Cataloging Division. *Subject Cataloging Manual: Subject Headings*. 3rd ed. Washington, D.C.: The Library, 1988. Sections H 1430 (Comics and Comic Characters), H 1610 (Fictitious Characters), H 1627 (Folklore Materials), H 1720 (Legends and Stories about Animals), H 1780 (Drama), H1790 (Fiction), H 1795 (Legends and Romances), and H 1800 (Poetry).

The Subject Analysis Committee recommends the provision of four kinds of subject access: form/genre access, access for characters or groups of characters, access for setting, and topical access. The following guidelines consist of instructions for providing these kinds of access.

History

In January of 1986, the Subject Analysis Committee of the Cataloging and Classification Section, Resources and Technical Services Division (now, Association for Library Collections and Technical Services), American Library Association, created the Subcommittee on Subject Access to Individual Works of Fiction, Drama, Etc. The Subcommittee was given the following charge:

To study LC subject headings and other subject heading lists, and recommend changes in LC subject cataloging policy and practice which would improve subject access to individual works of fiction, drama, poetry, humor, and folklore in all formats.

To create a set of guidelines to enable libraries to improve subject access to individual works of fiction, drama, poetry, humor, and folklore in all formats.

To study the MARC format and recommend changes in tagging and coding which would improve subject access to individual works of fiction, drama, poetry, humor, and folklore in all formats.

To study CIP practice and recommend changes which might ensure more timely subject access to these materials.

In the above charge, subject access is taken in its broadest sense to include access by way of genre/ form, fictional characters, groups, and places.

The Subcommittee met at every ALA Midwinter and Annual Conference from 1986 to 1989, consulted with interested individuals and institutions, and has produced the guidelines that follow. Members of the Subcommittee were:

Liz Bishoff, Chair
Barbara Berman
Bob Ihrig
Pat Luthin
Martha M. Yee

Library of Congress cooperative subject cataloging

The Library of Congress currently establishes subject headings only when needed by the Library of Congress. However, LC is encouraging cooperative subject cataloging. If you would like to have topical subject headings, or other headings useful for providing subject access to fiction, etc., added directly to *Library of Congress Subject Headings*, and if you will do the authority work necessary, you can propose new headings to LC for inclusion in *LCSH*. You must be willing to follow the guidelines specified in the *Subject Cataloging Manual: Subject Headings*.

If you would like to participate in this program, write to:

Chief,
Subject Cataloging Division
Library of Congress
Washington, D.C. 20540

She will send you reporting forms and a list of the parts of the *Subject Cataloging Manual: Subject Headings* that instruct you in how to fill out the forms.

Acknowledgements

Barbara Berman took on the considerable task of compiling and editing the Subcommittee's recommendations for these guidelines into a coherent whole, in addition to shouldering most of the burden of compiling the list of form/genre terms.

The Subcommittee would like particularly to acknowledge the help, constructive criticism, and encouragement it has received from the following individuals: Sandy Berman, Jan DeSirey, Christopher Dodge, Kay Elsasser, David Gleim, Peter Lisbon, Ichiko Morita, Mary Goss Mundy, Mary K.D. Pietris, Geoffrey Smith, Diane Parr Walker, and Paul Weiss. In addition, we would like to thank all the enthusiastic and helpful members of the audience who were so faithful in attendance at our meetings.

I. Form/genre access

Form/genre headings indicate what the work is, rather than what it is about. **Western stories**, for example, is used for the westerns themselves, rather than for works about westerns. Assign as many form/genre headings as appropriate.

The following list of headings is compiled primarily from the *Library of Congress Subject Headings (LCSH)*. In recommending these headings for individual works, however, we are in some cases not following Library of Congress (LC) rules of application. The list also includes several non-LC subject headings, especially for individual works of fiction (to which LC does not at present apply form headings) and for nonbook materials. The non-LC headings are indicated by footnotes. The appropriate field for form headings in the MARC format is 655. The second indicator should be set to 7, and a ≠2 subfield should be added to identify either these *Guidelines* or *LCSH*. Form headings found in *LCSH*, but omitted from the following list, may also be used; in this case the ≠2 subfield should identify *LCSH* as the source of the heading.

Legend

Boldface text – Preferred terms.

Lightface text – Nonpreferred terms.

BT – Broader term, see also.

RT – Related term, see also.

NT – Narrower term, see also.

List of form/genre headings

Adult fiction
> Use **Erotic stories**

Adult films
> Use **Erotic films**

Adventure films
> Used for Suspense films
>> Swashbucklers
>> Thrillers
>
> NT **Detective and mystery films**
>> **Science fiction films**
>> **Science fiction television programs**
>> **Spy films**
>> **Spy television programs**
>> **Western films**
>> **Westerns (Television programs)**
>
> RT **Adventure television programs**

Adventure radio programs[1]

Adventure stories
> Used for Suspense novels
>> Swashbucklers
>> Thrillers
>
> NT **Detective and mystery stories**
>> **Picaresque literature**
>> **Robinsonades**
>> **Romantic suspense novels**[1]
>> **Science fiction**
>> **Spy stories**
>> **Western stories**

Adventure television programs[1]
> NT **Detective and mystery television programs**
> RT **Adventure films**

Allegories
> Used for Cautionary tales and verse
>> Moral and philosophic stories
>> Morality tales
>
> RT **Fables**
>> **Parables**

---

1 Not an LC heading

Alternative histories[1] — Use for works featuring key changes in   historical
facts.
> BT   **Fantastic fiction**

Animated films
> Used for Cartoons, animated
> Motion picture cartoons
> Moving-picture cartoons

Animated television programs[1]

Anti-utopias
> Use   **Dystopias**

Anti-war films
> Use   **War films**

Anti-war poetry
> Use   **War poetry**

Anti-war stories
> Use   **War stories**

Apocalyptic fantasies
> Use   **Fantastic fiction**
> **Fantastic films**
> **Fantastic television programs**
> **Robinsonades**
> **Science fiction**
> **Science fiction films**
> **Science fiction plays**
> **Science fiction television programs**
> **War films**
> **War stories**

Apprenticeship novels
> Use   **Bildungsromane**[2]

Arthurian romances

Autobiographical fiction
> BT   **Biographical fiction**
> RT   **Historical fiction**

Bible films

---

1 Not an LC heading.
2 Not an LC heading. LC uses **Bildungsroman** (singular) for works *about* the genre.

Bible plays[1] — Use for dramatizations of biblical events.
> NT **Mysteries and miracle plays**
> **Passion plays**

Bildungsromane[2] — Use for novels in which the theme is the development of a character from youth to adulthood.
> Used for Apprenticeship novels
> Coming of age stories

Biographical fiction — Use for fictionalized accounts of the life of a real person.
> Used for Biographical novels
> NT **Autobiographical fiction**
> RT **Historical fiction**

Biographical films

Biographical novels
> Use **Biographical fiction**

Biographical radio programs[3]

Biographical television programs[3]

Black comedy (Literature)
> Use **Black humor (Literature)**[4]

Black humor (Literature)[4] — Use for works characterized by a desperate, sardonic humor intended to induce laughter as the appropriate response to the apparent meaninglessness and absurdity of existence.
> Used for Black comedy (Literature)
> Dark humor (Literature)

Bucolic poetry
> Use **Pastoral poetry**

Cartoons, animated
> Use **Animated films**

Cautionary tales and verse
> Use **Allegories**
> **Didactic fiction**
> **Didactic poetry**
> **Fables**
> **Parables**

---

1 LC uses only when a play is not entered under the name of a principal character or other specific heading.
2 Not an LC heading. LC uses **Bildungrsoman** (singular) for works *about* the genre.
3 Not an LC heading.
4 LC uses only for works *about* black humor.

Chap-books
    Used for Jest-books
    RT   **Comic books, strips, etc.**
Chronicle history (Drama)
    Use   **Historical drama**
Chronicle plays
    Use   **Historical drama**
Comedies[1]
    Used for Humorous plays
             Slapstick comedies
    NT   **Comedy films**
             Comedy radio programs[2]
             Comedy television programs[2]
Comedy films —Consult *LCSH* for specific kinds of comedy films: e.g.,
             Three Stooges films.
    Used for Humorous films
    BT   **Comedies**
    RT   **Comedy television programs**[2]
Comedy radio programs[2]
    Used for Radio comedy programs
Comedy television programs[2]
    Used for Sitcoms
             Situation comedies
             Slapstick comedies
             Television comedy programs
    BT   **Comedies**
    RT   **Comedy films**
Comic books, strips, etc.
    NT   **Detective and mystery comic books, strips, etc.**
             Science fiction comic books, strips, etc.
             Superhero comic books, strips, etc.[3]
             Western comic books, strips, etc.
    RT   **Chap-books**
Comic epic literature
    Use   **Mock-heroic literature**

---

1 Not an LC heading. LC uses the singular form, **Comedy**, for works *about* the genre.
2 Not an LC heading. LC uses the broader term, **Comedy programs**.
3 Not an LC heading.

Comic novels
> Use **Humorous stories**

Coming of age stories
> Use **Bildungsromane**[1]

Courtroom drama
> Use **Legal drama (Films)**[2]
> **Legal drama (Radio programs)**[2]
> **Legal drama (Television programs)**[2]

Creature films
> Use **Horror films**

Crime comics
> Use **Detective and mystery comic books, strips, etc.**

Crime films
> Use **Detective and mystery films**
> **Films noirs**
> **Gangster films**

Crime plays
> Use **Detective and mystery plays**

Crime programs
> Use **Detective and mystery radio programs**[2]
> **Detective and mystery television programs**

Crime stories
> Use **Detective and mystery stories**

Dark humor (Literature)
> Use **Black humor (Literature)**[3]

Detective and mystery comic books, strips, etc.
> Used for Crime comics
> Mystery and detective comics

Detective and mystery films —Consult *LCSH* for particular kinds of detective and mystery films: e.g., **Sherlock Holmes films.**
> Used for Crime films
> Murder mysteries
> Mysteries
> Mystery and detective films
> Private eye stories
> Suspense films
> Whodunits
> RT **Spy films**

---

1 Not an LC heading. LC uses **Bildungsroman** (singular) for works *about* the genre.
2 Not an LC heading.
3 LC uses only for works *about* black humor.

Detective and mystery plays
> Used for   Crime plays
>> Murder mysteries
>> Mysteries
>> Mystery and detective plays
>> Mystery plays
>> Private eye stories
>> Whodunits

Detective and mystery radio programs[1]
> Used for   Crime programs
>> Murder mysteries
>> Mysteries
>> Mystery and detective radio programs
>> Private eye stories
>> Suspense programs
>> Whodunits

Detective and mystery stories
> Used for   Crime stories
>> Murder mysteries
>> Mysteries
>> Mystery and detective stories
>> Mystery stories
>> Private eye stories
>> Suspense novels
>> Whodunits
>
> RT   **Ghost stories**
>> **Horror tales**
>> **Romantic suspense novels**[1]
>> **Spy stories**

Detective and mystery television programs
> Used for   Crime programs
>> Murder mysteries
>> Mysteries
>> Mystery and detective films
>> Mystery and detective television programs
>> Private eye stories
>> Suspense programs
>> Whodunits
>
> RT   **Spy television programs**

Didactic drama

Didactic fiction
> Used for   Cautionary tales and verse
>> Moral and philosophic stories
>> Morality tales
>
> NT   **Fables**
>> **Parables**

Didactic poetry
> Used for Cautionary tales and verse
> NT **Fables**
> **Parables**

Doctor films
> Use **Medical drama (Films)**[1]

Doctor novels
> Use **Medical novels**[1]

Doctor radio programs
> Use **Medical drama (Radio programs)**[1]

Doctor television programs
> Use **Medical drama (Television programs)**[1]

Dystopias
> Used for Anti-utopias
> BT **Fantastic fiction**
> **Science fiction**
> RT **Utopias**

Eclogues
> Use **Pastoral poetry**

Edwardian novels[1] —Use for historical novels set in the reign of Edward VII (1901–1909).
> BT **Historical fiction**

Elegiac poetry
> Used for Elegies
> Lamentations

Elegies
> Use **Elegiac poetry**

End-of-the-world fantasies
> Use **Fantastic fiction**
> **Fantastic films**
> **Fantastic television programs**
> **Robinsonades**
> **Science fiction**
> **Science fiction films**
> **Science fiction plays**
> **Science fiction television programs**
> **War films**
> **War stories**

Epic films[1]
> Used for Film epics

---

1 Not an LC heading.

Epic literature
> NT   **Epic poetry**
> RT   **Mock-heroic literature**

Epic poetry
> Used for   Heroic poetry
> BT   **Narrative poetry**
> NT   **Romances**

Epistolary fiction —Use for novels written in the form of a series of letters.
> Used for   Epistolary novels
>   Novels in letters

Epistolary novels
> Use   **Epistolary fiction**

Epistolary poetry
> Used for   Verse epistles

Erotic films
> Used for   Adult films

Erotic novels
> Use   **Erotic stories**

Erotic poetry
> RT   **Love poetry**

Erotic stories
> Used for   Adult fiction
>   Erotic novels
> RT   **Love stories**

Espionage films
> Use   **Spy films**

Espionage stories
> Use   **Spy stories**

Espionage television programs
> Use   **Spy television programs**

Fables
> Used for   Cautionary tales and verse
>   Moral and philosophic stories
> RT   **Allegories**
>   **Didactic fiction**
>   **Didactic poetry**
>   **Folklore**
>   **Legends**
>   **Parables**
>   **Romances**

Fairy tales
    BT   **Folklore**
Fantastic fiction
    Used for Apocalyptic fantasies
                 End-of-the-world fantasies
                 Fantasy
                 Time travel (Fiction)
    NT   **Alternative histories (Fiction)**[1]
             Dystopias
             Ghost stories
             Horror tales
             Occult fiction[1]
             Utopias
             Voyages, imaginary
    RT   **Interplanetary voyages**
             Science fiction
Fantastic films
    Used for Apocalyptic fantasies
                 End-of-the-world fantasies
                 Fantasy
                 Time travel (Fiction)
    NT   **Horror films**
    RT   **Science fiction films**
Fantastic poetry
Fantastic radio programs[1]
Fantastic television programs
    Used for Apocalyptic fantasies
                 End-of-the-world fantasies
                 Fantasy
                 Time travel (Fiction)
    RT   **Science fiction television programs**
Fantasy
    Use   **Fantastic fiction**
             Fantastic films
             Fantastic poetry
             Fantastic television programs
Farces
Feature films
Film epics
    Use   **Epic films**[1]

---

1 Not an LC heading.

Film scripts
    Use   **Motion picture plays**
Films noirs
    Used for Crime films
Filmscripts
    Use   **Motion picture plays**
Folk lore
    Use   **Folklore**
Folk tales
    Use   **Folklore**
                Legends
Folklore
    Used for Folk lore
                Folk tales
    NT   **Fables**
                Fairy tales
                Legends
                Tall tales
Gangster films
    Used for Crime films
Ghost stories
    Used for Terror tales
    BT   **Fantastic fiction**
                Occult fiction[1]
                Horror tales
    RT   **Gothic novels**[2]
Gothic novels[2] —Use for novels which have a medieval setting and which include castles and ghosts.
    BT   **Historical fiction**
                Horror tales
                Occult fiction
    RT   **Ghost stories**
                Love stories
                Romantic suspense novels[1]

---

[1] Not an LC heading.
[2] Not an LC heading. LC uses the singular form, **Gothic novel**, as cross-reference to the heading for works about the genre: **Gothic revival (Literature)**.

Historical drama
- Used for   Chronicle history (Drama)
- Chronicle plays
- NT   **Bible plays**[1]
- **War films**
- **Western films**
- **Westerns (Television programs)**

Historical fiction—Use for novels set during a time prior to the time in which they were written.
- Used for   Historical novels
- Historical romances
- NT   **Edwardian novels**[2]
- **Gothic novels**[3]
- **Regency novels**[2]
- **War stories**
- **Western stories**
- RT   **Autobiographical fiction**
- **Biographical fiction**

Historical novels
- Use   **Historical fiction**

Historical poetry
- BT   **Narrative poetry**

Historical romances
- Use   **Historical fiction**

Horror films —Consult *LCSH* for particular kinds of horror films: e.g., **Vampire films**.
- Used for   Creature films
- Monster films
- BT   **Fantastic films**

Horror novels
- Use   **Horror tales**

Horror plays
Horror radio programs

---

1 LC uses only when a play is not entered under the name of a principal character or other specific heading.

2 Not an LC heading.

3 Not an LC heading. LC uses the singular form, **Gothic novel**, as cross-reference to the heading for works about the genre: **Gothic revival (Literature)**.

Horror tales
>Used for Horror novels
>>Terror tales
>BT   **Fantastic fiction**
>NT   **Ghost stories**
>>**Gothic novels**[1]
>RT   **Occult fiction**[2]

Horror television programs
>BT   **Fantastic television programs**

Hospital novels
>Use   **Medical novels**[2]

Humor
>Use   **Wit and humor**

Humorous films
>Use   **Comedy films**

Humorous plays
>Use   **Comedies**

Humorous poetry
>Used for Humorous verse
>>Light verse

Humorous stories
>Used for Comic novels
>RT   **Mock-heroic literature**

Humorous verse
>Use   **Humorous poetry**

Idyllic poetry
>Use   **Pastoral poetry**

Imaginary voyages
>Use   **Voyages, imaginary**

Interplanetary voyages
>Used for Space flight (Fiction)
>RT   **Fantastic fiction**
>>**Science fiction**
>>**Voyages, imaginary**

Jest-books
>Use   **Chap-books**

Lamentations
>Use   **Elegiac poetry**

Legal drama (Films)[2]
>Used for Courtroom drama

---

1 Not an LC heading. LC uses the singular form, **Gothic novel**, as cross-reference to the heading for works about the genre: **Gothic revival (Literature)**.
2 Not an LC heading.

Legal drama (Radio programs)[1]
    Used for Courtroom drama
Legal drama (Television programs)[1]
    Used for Courtroom drama
Legal stories
Legends
    Used for Folk tales
    RT   **Fables**
             Folklore
             Romances
Light verse
    Use   **Humorous poetry**
Livres á clef —Use for novels in which the fictional characters and events
              can be identified with real persons and events.
    Used for Romans á clef
Love poetry
    RT   **Erotic poetry**
Love stories
    Used for Romances (Love stories)
    RT   **Erotic stories**
             Gothic novels[2]
             Romantic suspense novels[1]
Made-for-TV movies
    Use   **Television movies**[1]
Medical drama (Films)[1]
    Used for Doctor films
Medical drama (Radio programs)[1]
    Used for Doctor radio programs
Medical drama (Television programs)[1]
    Used for Doctor television programs
Medical novels[1] —Use for novels with a medical setting.
    Used for Doctor novels
               Hospital novels
Melodrama
Miracle plays
    Use   **Mysteries and miracle plays**
Mock epic literature
    Use   **Mock-heroic literature**

---

    1 Not an LC heading.
    2 Not an LC heading. LC uses the singular form, **Gothic novel**, as cross-reference to the heading for works about the genre: **Gothic revival (Literature)**.

Mock-heroic literature
> Used for Comic epic literature
>   Mock epic literature
> RT   **Epic literature**
>   **Humorous stories**

Monster films
> Use   **Horror films**

Moral and philosophic stories
> Use   **Allegories**
>   **Didactic fiction**
>   **Fables**
>   **Parables**

Moralities —Use for plays in which the chief characters are personifications
> of abstract qualities.
> Used for Morality plays
> RT   **Mysteries and miracle plays**

Morality plays
> Use   **Moralities**

Morality tales
> Use   **Allegories**
>   **Didactic fiction**
>   **Fables**
>   **Parables**

Motion picture cartoons
> Use   **Animated films**

Motion picture musicals
> Use   **Musical films**

Motion picture plays
> Used for Film scripts
>   Filmscripts
>   Screenplays

Motion picture serials

Movie novelizations
> Use   **Movie novels**[1]

Movie novels[1] —Use for novels based on movies.
> Used for Movie novelizations
>   Movie tie-ins
> RT   **Radio and television novels**[1]

Movie tie-ins
> Use   **Movie novels**[1]

---

1 Not an LC heading.

Moving-picture cartoons
    Use   **Animated films**
Moving-pictures, musical
    Use   **Musical films**
Murder mysteries
    Use   **Detective and mystery films**
             Detective and mystery plays
             Detective and mystery radio programs[1]
             Detective and mystery stories
             Detective and mystery television programs
Musical comedies
    Use   **Musical films**
Musical films
    Used for Motion picture musicals
               Moving pictures, musical
               Musicals (Motion pictures)
Musicals (Motion pictures)
    Use   **Musical films**
Mysteries
    Use   **Detective and mystery films**
             Detective and mystery plays
             Detective and mystery radio programs[1]
             Detective and mystery stories
             Detective and mystery television programs
             Mysteries and miracle plays
Mysteries and miracle plays —Use for medieval plays depicting the life of
             Christ or legends of the saints.
    Used for Miracle plays
               Mysteries
               Mystery plays
    BT   **Bible plays**[2]
    NT   **Passion plays**
    RT   **Moralities**
Mystery and detective comics
    Use   **Detective and mystery comic books, strips, etc.**
Mystery and detective films
    Use   **Detective and mystery films**
             Detective and mystery television programs

---

1 Not an LC heading.
2 LC uses only when a play is not entered under the name of a principal character or other specific heading.

Mystery and detective plays
> Use   **Detective and mystery plays**
> **Detective and mystery radio programs**[1]
> **Detective and mystery television programs**

Mystery and detective stories
> Use   **Detective and mystery stories**

Mystery plays
> Use   **Detective and mystery plays**
> **Mysteries and miracle plays**

Mystery stories
> Use   **Detective and mystery stories**

Narrative poetry
> NT   **Epic poetry**
> **Historical poetry**

Novels in letters
> Use   **Epistolary fiction**

Occult fiction[1]—Use for works about supernatural powers.
> BT   **Fantastic fiction**
> NT   **Ghost stories**
> **Gothic novels**[2]
> **Horror tales**

Parables
> Used for Cautionary tales and verse
> Moral and philosophic stories
> Morality tales
> RT   **Allegories**
> **Didactic fiction**
> **Didactic poetry**
> **Fables**

Passion plays —Use for medieval plays depicting the Passion of Christ.
> BT   **Bible plays**[3]
> **Mysteries and miracle plays**

Pastoral drama
> Used for Rural comedies

Pastoral fiction —Use for novels with a rural setting and a tone of romantic
> nostalgia.
> Used for Pastoral romances
> Rural comedies

---

1 Not an LC heading.

2 Not an LC heading. LC uses the singular form, **Gothic novel**, as cross-reference to the heading for works about the genre: **Gothic revival (Literature)**.

3 LC uses only when a play is not entered under the name of a principal character or other specific heading.

Pastoral poetry
> Used for Bucolic poetry
> Eclogues
> Idyllic poetry
> Rural poetry

Pastoral romances
> Use **Pastoral fiction**

Pastorals
> Use **Pastoral drama**
> **Pastoral fiction**
> **Pastoral poetry**

Picaresque literature —Use for episodic accounts of the adventures of an engagingly roguish hero.
> Used for Picaresque novels

Picaresque novels
> Use **Picaresque literature**

Private eye stories
> Use **Detective and mystery films**
> **Detective and mystery plays**
> **Detective and mystery radio programs**[1]
> **Detective and mystery stories**
> **Detective and mystery television programs**

Radio and television novels[1] —Use for novels based on radio or television programs.
> Used for Radio novels
> Television novels
> RT **Movie novels**[1]

Radio comedy programs
> Use **Comedy radio programs**[2]

Radio drama
> Use **Radio plays**

Radio novels
> Use **Radio and television novels**[1]

Radio plays
> Used for Radio drama
> NT **Soap operas**
> RT **Radio scripts**

Radio scripts
> RT **Radio plays**

Radio serials
> RT **Soap operas**

---

1 Not an LC heading.
2 Not an LC heading. LC uses the broader term, **Comedy Programs**.

Regency novels[1] —Use for historical novels set during the period when the future George IV acted as Regent for George III (ca. 1810–1820).

    BT   **Historical fiction**

Robinsonades —Use for works describing an individual's survival without the aid of civilization, as on a deserted island.

    Used for Apocalyptic fantasies

                  End-of-the-world fantasies

    BT   **Adventure stories**

              Voyages, imaginary

Romances —Use for medieval tales which embody the life and adventures of a hero of chivalry. For contemporary novels, use **Love stories** or **Romantic suspense novels.**

    NT   **Arthurian romances**

    RT   **Epic poetry**

              Fables

              Legends

Romances (Love stories)

    Use   **Love stories**

Romans á clef

    Use   **Livres á clef**

Romantic suspense novels[1] —Use for contemporary works. Medieval tales are entered under **Romances.**

    Used for Suspense novels

    RT   **Adventure stories**

              Detective and mystery stories

              Gothic novels[2]

              Love stories

              Spy stories

Rural comedies

    Use   **Pastoral drama**

              Pastoral fiction

Rural poetry

    Use   **Pastoral poetry**

---

1 Not an LC heading.

2 Not an LC heading. LC uses the singular form, **Gothic novel**, as cross-reference to the heading for works about the genre: **Gothic revival (Literature)**.

Science fiction —Use for works based on imagined developments in science and technology.

    Used for Apocalyptic fantasies

               End-of-the-world fantasies

               Space flight (Fiction)

               Time travel (Fiction)

    NT   **Dystopias**

               Utopias

               Voyages, imaginary

    RT   **Fantastic fiction**

               Interplanetary voyages

Science fiction comic books, strips, etc.

Science fiction films —Consult *LCSH* for particular kinds of science fiction films: e.g., **Star Trek films.**

Science fiction plays

    Used for Time travel (Fiction)

Science fiction poetry

Science fiction radio programs [1]

    Used for Time travel (Fiction)

Science fiction television programs

    Used for Time travel (Fiction)

Screenplays

    Use   **Motion picture plays**

               Television scripts

Short films

Silent films

Sitcoms

    Use   **Comedy television programs**[2]

Situation comedies

    Use   **Comedy television programs**[2]

Slapstick comedies

    Use   **Comedies**

               Comedy films

               Comedy television programs[2]

Soap operas

    BT   **Radio plays**

               Television plays

    RT   **Radio serials**

               Television serials

---

1 Not an LC heading.

2 Not an LC heading. LC uses the broader term, **Comedy Programs.**

Space flight (Fiction)
> Use **Interplanetary voyages**
> **Science fiction**
> **Voyages, imaginary**

Sports drama (Films)[1]
Sports drama (Radio programs)[1]
Sports drama (Television programs)[1]
Sports stories —Consult *LCSH* for particular kinds of sports stories: e.g.,
> **Baseball stories.**

Spy films
> Used for Espionage films
> Suspense films
> RT **Detective and mystery films**

Spy novels
> Use **Spy stories**

Spy radio programs[1]
Spy stories
> Used for Espionage stories
> Spy novels
> RT **Detective and mystery stories**
> **Romantic suspense novels**[1]

Spy television programs
> Used for Espionage television programs
> Suspense programs
> RT **Detective and mystery television programs**

Subterranean voyages
> Use **Voyages, Imaginary**

Superhero comic books, strips, etc.[1]
Superhero films[1] —Consult *LCSH* for films with particular superheroes:
> e.g., **Superman films.**

Superhero radio programs[1]
Superhero television programs[1]
Suspense films
> Use **Adventure films**
> **Detective and mystery films**
> **Spy films**

Suspense novels
> Use **Adventure stories**
> **Detective and mystery stories**
> **Spy stories**
> **Romantic suspense novels**[1]

---

1 Not an LC heading.

Suspense programs
>Use **Detective and mystery radio programs**
>   **Detective and mystery television programs**
>   **Spy television programs**

Swashbucklers
>Use **Adventure films**
>   **Adventure stories**

Tall tales
>BT **Folklore**

Television comedy programs
>Use **Comedy television programs**[1]

Television drama
>Use **Television plays**

Television films
>Use **Television movies**[2]

Television movies[2]
>Used for Made-for-TV movies
>   Television films

Television novels
>Use **Radio and television novels**[2]

Television plays
>Used for Television drama
>NT **Soap operas**
>RT **Television scripts**

Television scripts
>Used for Screenplays
>RT **Television plays**

Television serials
>RT **Soap operas**

Terror tales
>Use **Ghost stories**
>   **Horror tales**

Thrillers
>Use **Adventure films**
>   **Adventure stories**

---

1 Not an LC heading. LC uses the broader term, **Comedy Programs.**
2 Not an LC heading.

Time travel (Fiction)
    Use   **Fantastic fiction**
               Fantastic films
               Fantastic television programs
               Science fiction
               Science fiction films
               Science fiction plays
               Science fiction radio programs[1]
               Science fiction television programs
               Voyages, imaginary

Tragedies[2]
Utopias
    BT   **Fantastic fiction**
               Science fiction
    RT   **Dystopias**
Variety films[1]
Variety shows (Radio programs)[1]
Variety shows (Television programs)
Verse epistles
    Use   **Epistolary poetry**
Voyages, imaginary
    Used for Imaginary voyages
                   Space flight (Fiction)
                   Subterranean voyages
                   Time travel (Fiction)
                   Voyages to the moon
    NT   **Robinsonades**
    BT   **Fantastic fiction**
               Science fiction
    RT   **Interplanetary voyages**
Voyages to the moon
    Use   **Voyages, imaginary**
War films
    Used for Anti-war films
                   Apocalyptic fantasies
                   End-of-the-world fantasies
    RT   **Historical drama**
War poetry
    Used for Anti-war poetry
War radio programs[1]

---

1 Not an LC heading.
2 Not an LC heading. LC uses the singular form, **Tragedy,** for works *about* the genre.

War stories
> Used for Anti-war stories
> Apocalyptic fantasies
> End-of-the-world fantasies
> RT **Historical fiction**

War television programs[1]

Western comic books, strips, etc.

Western films —Consult *LCSH* for particular kinds of western films: e.g., **Lone Ranger films**
> Used for Westerns
> BT **Adventure films**
> **Historical drama**

Western stories —Use for post–19th-century works set in the 19th-century American West.
> Used for Westerns
> BT **Adventure stories**
> **Historical fiction**

Westerns
> Use **Western films**
> **Western stories**
> **Westerns (Radio programs)**[1]
> **Westerns (Television programs)**

Westerns (Radio programs)[1]
> Used for Westerns

Westerns (Television programs)
> Used for Westerns

Whodunits
> Use **Detective and mystery films**
> **Detective and mystery plays**
> **Detective and mystery radio programs**[1]
> **Detective and mystery stories**
> **Detective and mystery television programs**

Wit and humor
> Used for Humor
> NT **Black humor (Literature)**[2]
> **Chap-books**
> **Comedies**
> **Comic books, strips, etc.**
> **Humorous poetry**
> **Humorous stories**
> **Mock-heroic literature**
> **Tall tales**

---

1 Not an LC heading.
2 LC uses only for works *about* black humor.

II. Character access

Introduction

As indicated in the general introduction, the guidelines below are not designed to apply to works *about* characters, which is out of our scope, but rather to provide subject access for characters in works of fiction, drama, etc.

Fictitious characters

Assign headings for fictitious and legendary characters and groups to individual works of fiction, drama, poetry, humor, folklore, and music, providing that they appear prominently in three or more different works. Add an appropriate parenthetical qualifier from the following list:

(Fictitious character)

(Legendary character)

([Nationality] deity), e.g. (Greek deity)

([Nationality] mythology), e.g. (Greek mythology)

Use more specific qualifiers only when needed to resolve a conflict or when ambiguity might result from use of a more general qualifier.

EXAMPLES: **Thor (Cartoon character)**

Thor (Norse deity)

Add an appropriate form subdivision. The subdivisions recommended below constitute a new list designed specifically for use with names of characters. As such, it does not correspond to the list of free-floating subdivisions to be used under the names of persons, as detailed in the LC subject manual.

Art	Juvenile drama	Operas*
Caricatures and cartoons	Juvenile fiction	Pictorial works
Comic books, strips, etc.	Juvenile films	Poetry
Computer files	Juvenile humor	Posters
Drama	Juvenile poetry	Romances
Fiction	Juvenile sound recordings	Sermons
Folklore	Legends	Slides
Humor	Musicals*	Songs and music
		Statues

EXAMPLES: **Holmes, Sherlock (Fictitious character)—Fiction.**
Bugs Bunny (Fictitious character)—Juvenile films.

Use the form of name that appears in *LCSH*. If the name is not an LC heading, accept the form in the Hennepin County (Minnesota) Public Library authority file. If it is not there, establish it as follows.

If the name varies, consult other works featuring the character or group, and then appropriate reference works, to determine the commonly used form. Prefer a commonly known form of the name in English, if there is one. If there is not, prefer the commonly used form of the name in English language reference sources. If the name cannot be found in reference sources, establish the name based on the work in hand. A bibliography of appropriate reference works is attached as an Appendix. Follow practices in *AACR2*, Chapters 22–24, to determine forms of name for fictitious persons with terms of nobility, corporate bodies with subdivisions, and other such special problems.

Character with surname. Establish in inverted form all characters whose names include a surname. Add as a final element of the name any titles of address associated with the name.

EXAMPLES: **Shore, Jemima (Fictitious character)**
Wimsey, Peter, Lord (Fictitious character)
Collins, Mr. (Fictitious character)
Boop, Betty (Fictitious character)
Bunyan, Paul (Legendary character)

---

*Subdivisions not yet in LCSH. If one of these is used, the resultant heading should be placed in a 690 field in the MARC format.

Character with forename or nickname. Establish a character known by forename only or by nickname directly under that name. Add an appropriate parenthetical qualifier from the same list as for characters with surnames.

EXAMPLES: **Fabiano (Fictitious character)**
Little Orphan Annie (Fictitious character)
Bugs Bunny (Fictitious character)
John Henry (Legendary character)
Scheherazade (Legendary character)
Aphrodite (Greek deity)
Achilles (Greek mythology)

Named groups of characters. Establish named groups of fictitious or legendary characters according to the same pattern as individual characters. Use plural parenthetical qualifiers.

EXAMPLES: **Hardy Boys (Fictitious characters)**
Sartoris family (Fictitious characters)
Muses (Greek deities)

Corporate bodies. Establish fictitious corporate bodies using the parenthetical qualifier (Imaginary organization).

EXAMPLES: **SMERSH (Imaginary organization)**
Great Britain. Circumlocution Office (Imaginary organization)

References. Make UF (see) references from other names by which the character or group may be known, including uninverted forms for characters entered under surname.

EXAMPLE: **Shadow (Fictitious character)**
      UF   Cranston, Lamont (Fictitious character)
              Lamont Cranston (Fictitious character)
              The Shadow (Fictitious character)

Make BT (Broader term, see also) references from the appropriate medium to which the character is related. For literary characters, make a BT reference from **Characters and characteristics in literature.**

EXAMPLES: **Snoopy (Fictitious character)**
      BT   **Comic books, strips, etc.**
Pantaloon (Fictitious character)
      BT   **Commedia dell'arte**
             Pantomime
Cock Robin (Fictitious character)
      BT   **Characters and characteristics in literature**

Real persons

Assign headings for real persons which appear as characters in individual works of fiction, drama, poetry, humor, folklore, and music. Following LC practice, assign the name as found in the name authority file, with appropriate form subdivision. However, if the person is best known as a literary author, use the following form instead: [Name], in fiction, drama, poetry, etc.

EXAMPLES: **Lincoln, Abraham, 1809–1865—Juvenile drama.**
Veronica, Saint, 1st century—Legends.
Noah (Biblical figure)—Drama.
Dickinson, Emily, 1830–1886, in fiction, drama, poetry, etc.

III. Setting access

When appropriate, bring out location and time period (setting) by means of subject headings. For settings which correspond to real places, assign the place name as found in the name authority file, with one of the following form subdivisions.

Drama	Juvenile drama	Juvenile poetry
Fiction	Juvenile fiction	Juvenile sound recordings
Folklore	Juvenile films	Legends
Humor	Juvenile humor	Poetry
		Romance

For fictitious places which appear in at least three different works, assign the name as it appears in *LCSH,* with one of the above form subdivisions. If the name is not an LC heading, accept the form in the Hennepin County (Minnesota) Public Library authority file. If it is not there, establish the name as indicated below. Fictitious places use the parenthetical qualifier (Imaginary place). If the fictitious place is not in *LCSH,* put it in a 690 field in the MARC format.

If the fictitious place name varies, consult other works featuring the place, and then appropriate reference works to determine the most commonly used form. Prefer a commonly known form of name in English, if there is one. If there is not, prefer the commonly used form of name in English language reference sources. If the name cannot be found in reference sources, establish it based on the work in hand. A bibliography of appropriate reference works is attached as the Appendix. Use *AACR2*, Chapter 23, for jurisdictional names, or the subject cataloging manual for other place names to determine the form in which a place name should be established.

EXAMPLES: **Paris (France)—Poetry.**
United States—History—Civil War, 1861–1864—Drama.
Grand Fenwick (Imaginary place)—Fiction.
Middle Earth (Imaginary place)—Fiction.
Narnia (Imaginary place)—Fiction.
Yoknapatawpha County (Imaginary place)—Fiction.

IV. Topical access

Assign as many topical subject headings as necessary to bring out the topic(s) covered, as determined after a superficial review of the publication in hand. Do not attempt to discern topics which have not been made explicit by the author or publisher, or which could be interpreted as representing value judgments.

Add one of the subdivisions listed under Setting to each topical heading:

EXAMPLES: **Physicians—Fiction.**
                Christmas—Juvenile poetry.
                Dragons—Legends.

Appendix

BIBLIOGRAPHY OF SOURCES FOR FICTITIOUS CHARACTER AND PLACE NAMES

Bordman, Gerald. *Oxford companion to American theatre.* New York: Oxford Univ. Press, 1984.

    Under authors and theatrical works, characters are mentioned in plot summaries; no entries under characters.

Brewer, Ebenezer Cobham. *Brewer's dictionary of phrase and fable.* Centenary ed., rev. by Ivor H. Evans. New York: Harper, 1981.

    Includes fictitious, mythological, and legendary characters.

Concise Oxford dictionary of French literature. Joyce M.H. Reid, ed. Oxford: Clarendon Press, 1976.

    Lists authors and works, but has cross references from fictitious characters to their authors.

Cottrill, Tim; Greenberg, Martin H.; Waugh, Charles G. *Science fiction and fantasy series and sequels: A bibliography.* New York: Garland, 1986–

    The sequence index, on p. 285–305 in v. 1, lists many fictitious characters and imaginary places.

Detectionary: A biographical dictionary of leading characters in detective and mystery fiction, including famous and little-known sleuths, their helpers, rogues, both heroic and sinister, and some of their most memorable adventures, as recounted in novels, short stories, and films. Otto Penzler, et al., comps. Woodstock, N.Y.: Overlook Press, 1977.

    Title is self-descriptive; listings are in four sequences: 1) detectives; 2) rogues and helpers; 3) cases; and 4) movies. Radio and television programs are covered, as well as films. Under characters' names, the names of creators are given, the character is described, and the character's relationship to other characters is delineated.

Dictionary of famous names in fiction, drama, poetry, history, and art. Johnson, Rossiter, ed. Detroit: Gale, 1974.

Entries alphabetically arranged, with short descriptions; no author index. Includes some fictitious places.

Dictionary of Italian literature. Peter Bondanella and Julia Conaway Bondanella, co-editors. Westport, Conn.: Greenwood, 1979.

Under authors, characters are mentioned in plot summaries. No entries under the characters.

East, Andy. *The cold war file.* Metuchen, N.J.: Scarecrow, 1983.

Includes a one-page "secret agent index" (p. 361) to full entries under authors of spy novels of the 1960's; entries give the characters' various names, histories, and relationships to other characters.

Elkhadem, Saad. *The York companion to themes and motifs of world literature: Mythology, history, and folklore.* Fredericton, N.B.: York Press, 1981.

Many mythological, biblical, legendary and literary characters are listed, with descriptions of their stories and relationships to other characters, and citations to works.

Encyclopedia of frontier and western fiction. Jon Tuska and Vicki Piekarski, editors-in-chief. New York: McGraw-Hill, 1983.

For the most part, fictitious characters are listed and described under their authors; there are some fictitious character cross–references to author names, but not all are referenced.

Encyclopedia of mystery and detection. Chris Steinbrunner and Otto Penzler, editors-in-chief. New York: McGraw-Hill, 1976.

Includes extensive entries on well-known fictitious characters; describes characters and their relationships to other characters, and lists works, including books, films, and radio and television programs.

Encyclopedie des bandes dessinees. Paris: Albin Michel, 1978.

In French: encyclopedia of comic strips. International in scope; cross references from major characters to their creators, and an index which includes characters. Illustrated.

Fisher, Margery T. *Who's who in children's books: A treasury of the familiar characters of childhood.* New York: Holt, 1975.

Lists characters, with their histories, authors, and work(s).

Freeman, William. *Everyman's dictionary of fictional characters*. Rev. by Fred Urquhart. Boston: The Writer, 1985.

> Most valuable for characters in English and American novels, short stories, poems, and plays. Lists characters, explains their relationships to other characters, and cites author(s), and work(s).

Funk & Wagnall's standard dictionary of folklore, mythology, and legend. Maria Leach, ed. San Francisco: Harper, 1984, c1972.

> Includes deities, mythological and biblical figures, and folk heroes.

Gifford, Denis. *Encyclopedia of comic characters*. Burnt Mill, Harlow, Essex, England: Longman, 1987.

> Includes comic book characters.

_____. *The golden age of radio: An illustrated companion*. London: B.T.Batsford, 1985.

> This encyclopedia of British radio programs spanning "the thirties to the fifties, but not too strictly" includes entries under fictional characters alphabetically by first name.

Hagen, Ordean A. *Who done it? a guide to detective, mystery and suspense fiction*. New York: Bowker, 1969.

> Lists film detectives and the actors who have played them, beginning on p. 465. Includes an alphabetical list of detective, mystery and suspense characters, with author and a representative title, beginning on p. 497.

HCL authority file. Minnetonka, Minn.: Hennepin County Library Technical Services Division, 1977- [microfiche].

> Includes all fictitious characters and imaginary places established by the Hennepin County Public Library, including cross references from variant forms.

Hubin, Allen J. *Crime fiction, 1749–1975: A comprehensive bibliography*. New York: Garland, 1984.

> "Series index" beginning on p. 689 lists characters, and gives names of authors. This may be the most exhaustive work for this genre.

Johnson, Clifford R. *Plots and characters in the fiction of eighteenth–century English authors*. Folkestone, England: Dawson, 1977-1978.

> Title is self-explanatory.

Keating, H.R.F. *Whodunit? A guide to crime, suspense, and spy fiction*. New York: Van Nostrand Reinhold, 1982.

> Includes an alphabetical list of prominent fictitious characters with description and the names of their creators, beginning on p. 249.

Magill, Frank N. *Cyclopedia of literary characters.* New York: Harper, 1963.

> Includes 16,000 characters from 1300 novels, dramas, and epics. Entries arranged by title of work; includes principal characters and plot synopses; international in scope, it covers the literary classics. Includes a character index, and an author index. Very useful.

Manguel, Alberto. *The dictionary of imaginary places.* Expanded ed. San Diego: Harcourt, 1987.

> Includes full descriptions of each place, maps, and other illustrations. Entries are arranged alphabetically, with cross references for variant names; includes an index of authors and titles. A first rate source.

Naha, Ed. *Horrors: From screen to scream; An encyclopedic guide to the greatest horror and fantasy films of all time.* New York: Avon, 1975.

> Lists films by title with an occasional separate entry for a fictitious character. Useful because many films were called by the names of horror and fantasy characters.

_____. *The science fictionary.* 1st ed. New York: Seaview Bks., 1980.

> Characters are not listed directly, but are mentioned under the titles of films and television programs, and under the writers of science fiction.

Olderr, Steven. *Mystery index: Subjects, settings, and sleuths of 10,000 titles.* Chicago: American Library Assn., 1987.

> Includes a character index with names of authors (p. 463-492).

Oxford companion to English literature. 5th ed. Margaret Drabble, ed. Oxford: Oxford Univ. Press, 1985.

> Lists prominent characters from English fiction; includes their histories and the authors and titles of works in which they figure.

Oxford companion to Spanish literature. Philip Ward, ed. Oxford: Clarendon Press, 1978.

> Under authors and literary works, characters are mentioned in plot summaries; no direct access under character names.

Oxford companion to the theatre. 4th ed. Ed. by Phyllis Hartnoll. London: Oxford Univ. Press, 1983.

> Contains entries for a few famous theatrical characters (e.g. Punch and Judy, Pierrot), with a history and description of each.

Palmer, Robin. *A dictionary of mythical places.* New York: H.Z. Walck, 1975.

> Alphabetically arranged, cross-referenced dictionary of mythical, legendary, and famous literary places briefly described.

Pickard, Roy. *Who played who in the movies*: *A–Z*. New York: Schocken, 1981, c1979.

> An alphabetical list of characters (including real as well as fictitious people); each entry describes the character, indicates the original creator of a fictitious character, and lists the actors/actresses who have played the character, together with film title and date.

Ramsdell, Kristin. *Happily ever after: a guide to reading interests in romance fiction*. Littleton, Colo.: Libraries Unlimited, 1987.

> In separate categories by genre, authors and works are listed, including some plot synopses and character names. Characters are not indexed, but authors are.

Rovin, Jeff. *The encyclopedia of superheroes*. New York: Facts on File Publications, 1985.

> An alphabetical list of superheroes in comic books, films, television and radio. Each entry describes the character, gives the names of "alter egos," and gives a citation to the initial appearance of the character, with date. Includes index.

Sharp, Harold S. and Sharp, Marjorie Z.. *Index to characters in the performing arts*. New York: Scarecrow, 1966–1973.

> Covers characters in both musical and nonmusical plays, ballets, and radio and television. Within those categories, characters are listed alphabetically, entries explain relationships with other characters, and cite author(s), and work(s).

Smith, Myron J. *Cloak and dagger fiction: An annotated guide to spy thrillers*. Santa Barbara, Calif.: ABC-Clio, 1982.

> A list of fictitious characters, with authors' names, begins on p.375.

Swan, Helena. *Who's who in fiction? A dictionary of noted names in novels, tales, romances, poetry, and drama*. Detroit: Gale, 1906 (1975 reprint).

> Lists characters from English novels, poems and plays, as well as the Arabian nights, and medieval romances of chivalry.

The world encyclopedia of cartoons. Maurice Horn, ed. New York: Gale, 1980.

> Includes listings for major cartoon characters from newspapers, comic books and animated cartoons. The index leads to other characters mentioned in entries under cartoonists and animators.